Wildlife Watching

# Deer Watching

**by Diane Bair and Pamela Wright**

**Consultant:**
Brian P. Murphy
Executive Director
Quality Deer Management Association

CAPSTONE BOOKS
an imprint of Capstone Press
Mankato, Minnesota

W9-CBC-398

Capstone Books are published by Capstone Press
P.O. Box 669, 151 Good Counsel Drive, Mankato, Minnesota 56002
http://www.capstone-press.com

Copyright © 2000 Capstone Press. All rights reserved.
No part of this book may be reproduced without written permission from the publisher.
The publisher takes no responsibility for the use of any of the materials or methods
described in this book, nor for the products thereof.
Printed in the United States of America.

*Library of Congress Cataloging-in-Publication Data*
Bair, Diane.
    Deer watching/Diane Bair and Pamela Wright.
    p. cm.—(Wildlife watching)
    Includes bibliographical references and index.
    Summary: Describes some of the different species of North American deer, their
characteristics and habits, and how to go about observing them.
    ISBN 0-7368-0321-1
    1. Deer watching—Juvenile literature. [1. Deer. 2. Wildlife watching.]
I. Wright, Pamela, 1953– . II. Title. III. Series: Bair, Diane. Wildlife watching.
QL737.U55B316 2000
599.65–DC21
                                                                  99-14651
                                                                 CIP

**Editorial Credits**
Carrie A. Braulick, editor; Steve Christensen, cover designer and illustrator;
    Heidi Schoof, photo researcher

**Photo Credits**
Colephoto/John Flower, 4; Mary Clay, 7
David F. Clobes, cover inset, 12, 17, 20, 23, 30, 39
Dominique Braud/TOM STACK & ASSOCIATES, 34
Index Stock Imagery, 8
International Stock/Scott Barrow, cover
Kent and Donna Dannen, 18
Robert McCaw, 24, 27
Thomas Kitchin/TOM STACK & ASSOCIATES, 15, 36, 43 (top)
Unicorn Stock Photos/Ted Rose, 33 (bottom), 40
Uniphoto, 42
Visuals Unlimited/Leonard Lee Rue III, 11; John Sohlden, 22; Milton H. Tierney, Jr.,
    33 (top); Joe McDonald, 41; Rod Kieft, 43 (bottom)

**Thank you to Richard McCabe, Wildlife Management Institute, for his assistance
in preparing this book.**

# Table of Contents

## Chapter 1

# Getting to Know Deer

Deer are one of the most common wild animals in North America. Most people have encountered deer. This is because deer can adapt. They change their habits to fit their surroundings. Many deer live near people. You may find deer near your home.

### About Deer

About 50 types of deer live in the world. Each type of deer is called a species. Five deer species live in North America. These are elk, moose, caribou, white-tailed deer, and mule deer. Caribou sometimes are called reindeer.

**Deer can adapt to their surroundings.**

The two most common North American deer species are white-tailed deer and mule deer. This book mainly deals with these two deer species.

Deer species share some common features. Deer have narrow heads, large ears, and short tails. They have hoofs. Deer have stomachs with four parts to help them digest food.

Some deer have excellent running and jumping abilities. These deer may run as fast as 40 miles (64 kilometers) per hour. They may jump more than 7 feet (2.1 meters) high from a standing position. They may jump more than 8 feet (2.4 meters) high when running.

## Antlers

Antlers are a pair of bone growths on the heads of bucks. Bucks are male deer more than 1 year old. Antlers fall off each winter. Bucks then grow a new set of antlers. Does do not grow antlers. Does are female deer more than 1 year old.

Soft, short fur covers deer antlers as they grow. This fur is called velvet. Velvet falls off when deer antlers are finished growing.

**Deer have narrow heads and large ears.**

**Deer use their antlers to challenge each other.**

Each deer's antlers are unique. Older deer usually have larger antlers than younger deer. Healthy deer often have larger antlers than unhealthy deer.

Antlers are important during the fall and winter breeding seasons. Bucks often challenge each other during these months. They may use their antlers to fight. Bucks with the largest bodies and antlers usually win. These deer then are more likely to mate.

## Home Ranges and Migration

Deer travel through areas of land to search for food and to mate. These areas are called home ranges. Most North American deer have small home ranges. A mule deer's home range is usually about one-half square mile to 13 square miles (1.3 to 34 square kilometers). A white-tailed deer's home range is about 1 square mile (2.6 square kilometers).

Bucks and does live differently in their home ranges. Most bucks live alone. Does often share their home ranges with other does and fawns. Fawns are deer less than 1 year old. Bucks and does may share home ranges during winter. Food often is scarce during this time. Deer gather in feeding areas to share available food.

Deer that live in cold climates may migrate during early winter. They move to different areas to find food. These areas are called winter ranges. They return to their summer ranges during spring. Deer in warmer climates seldom migrate. These deer often can find food in the same place year-round.

## Important Animals
Deer were important animals to people in the past. American Indians and European settlers hunted deer for food. They also used deer skins to make clothing. Some European settlers traded deer skins for other food and supplies.

People still eat deer meat today. This meat is called venison. Many people hunt wild deer. Others raise certain deer species on deer farms for food.

**Does often live with their fawns.**

*Chapter 2*

# Preparing for Your Adventure

Learn about deer before you go deer watching. Check out books about deer from your local school or library. You may want to study a field guide. Field guides show what animals look like and tell where they live. This book has a short field guide on pages 40 to 43. Field guides can help you learn about deer species in your area.

## When to Go
Spring and summer are good seasons to watch deer. Does raise their fawns during these months. You may see deer feed on the plentiful plants.

**Gather supplies to prepare for deer watching.**

It is best not to go deer watching during fall. Hunting season begins in fall. You could be hurt by hunters who do not see you. Deer also may be hard to observe during fall. Deer sometimes become uneasy during this time of year. They may be more likely to run away from unfamiliar objects, noises, or smells.

You may observe deer during fall in areas where deer are protected. Some national parks and wildlife refuges do not permit deer hunting. Talk to rangers to make sure hunting is not allowed before you watch deer in these areas. Rangers are people in charge of parks or forests.

Early mornings and evenings are the best times to see deer. Deer search for food during these times. They usually rest during the day. But they may hunt for food during the day in winter.

**What to Bring**
Bring a pair of binoculars when you go deer watching. Binoculars make distant objects

**You can watch deer during fall in protected areas.**

appear closer. You easily can observe deer with binoculars.

Bring along items to record what you see. You may want to bring a camera with a telephoto lens. These lenses allow you to view and take photographs of distant objects. Bring a notebook and pencils, pens, or markers. You may want to bring a field guide.

Other supplies also may be useful for deer watching. You may want to bring plaster of paris. You can make casts of deer tracks with plaster of paris. Mix this white powder with a small amount of water to form a paste. Put the paste in deer tracks. Wait until the plaster hardens and carefully dig it out. You can buy plaster of paris at most art supply or craft stores. A ruler also may be helpful to measure tracks.

Take all of your supplies home. Pick up your litter when you leave. Litter can choke animals and pollute the environment.

## What to Wear

Wear soft-soled shoes when you watch deer. This will help decrease the noise you make. Deer have excellent hearing. Deer probably will run away if they hear you coming.

Do not wear scented products such as deodorant and perfume. Deer may smell the scents and run away.

**You may want to use a camera with a telephoto lens to record your observations.**

**Deer sometimes live near people's homes.**

Wear clothing that blends into the surroundings. This will make it more difficult for deer to see you. Wear light brown or green clothes during the summer. These colors will help you blend in with plants. Wear gray or light-colored clothes during the winter. This clothing will help you blend in with the colors of bare trees and snow.

Some types of clothing can protect you. Always wear long-sleeved shirts and pants. This will help protect you from insect bites. Dress warmly during winter for protection from the cold. Wear gloves or mittens to protect your hands. A hat or hood will keep your head and ears warm. Wear warm boots and heavy socks to protect your feet.

## Stay Hidden

Try to hide from deer. Deer that sense you probably will run away. Crouch behind bushes or trees. Be as still as you can. Deer cannot see still objects very well. But they can detect slight movement. Move very slowly if you move to another area.

You can prevent deer from sensing you in other ways. Walk into the wind. The wind will then blow your scent away from deer ahead of you. You may want to build a blind. A blind is a place where people can hide from animals. You can learn how to build a blind on page 22 of this book.

## Safety

Make sure to stay safe when you go deer watching. Children should bring an adult to guide them. Stay on marked trails. You may destroy plants or become lost if you wander off trails.

Deer sometimes live on private land. Get permission from all landowners before you go deer watching on their land.

You also should behave in ways that protect deer. Try not to startle deer. Do not talk loudly or run toward them. Startled deer might get hurt jumping over fences or other objects.

**Adults can guide children when they look for deer.**

STONY CREEK
ELEMENTARY LIBRARY

# Build a Blind

Blinds can help you watch deer closely. They keep you hidden from deer. You can build several different types of blinds. Here is one simple type of blind you can make.

**1.** Find a place to build your blind. Look for an area in the woods with many trees and other plants to hide your blind. You may want to place your blind near an open area. This will allow you to watch deer that are far away.

**2.** Set up a blind at least one week before you plan to use it. This helps deer become used to the blind. Deer are more likely to come near the blind if it is a familiar object.

**3.** Find a log, stump, bush, or large rock to support your blind.

**4.** Gather large branches from the ground. Place these branches in a line or semicircle around the log, stump, bush, or rock. Leave small openings between the branches.

**5.** You may want to put grass, leaves, or other brush on your blind. This makes your blind blend into the surroundings.

**6.** Remove the leaves and twigs from the ground in and around your blind. Leaves and twigs make noise if you step on them. This noise can startle deer.

**7.** Peek out through openings between the branches to see deer.

## Chapter 3

# Where to Look

Look for deer in their habitats. These are the natural places and conditions in which deer live. White-tailed deer live in forests, open fields, and meadows. These deer may live near people. Mule deer live in most habitats except very dry deserts. They often live in hilly or mountainous areas.

You also can look for deer species in their ranges. These are the geographic regions where a plant or animal species naturally lives. Some deer have a wide North American range. For example, white-tailed deer live throughout most of North America. Other deer have a smaller North American range. Caribou only live in the northern part of the continent.

**Mule deer often live in mountainous habitats.**

## Feeding Areas

Look for deer near their feeding areas. Deer are browsers. They eat tender shoots of plants. These plants may include shrubs and trees. You may see deer near fruit orchards. Deer eat fruit that has fallen on the ground. Deer sometimes feed on plants in people's gardens or crops in fields. Look for deer near rivers or streams. Deer visit these areas to drink water.

You may see deer traveling to and from their feeding areas. Deer usually feed in open areas. They then go back to the forest to rest. Forests hide deer from predators such as wolves, coyotes, and bobcats. Predators hunt other animals for food.

Deer often have regular feeding areas. Return to feeding areas where you have seen deer before. The same deer may be there again. Deer usually travel the same paths to and from their feeding areas.

**Deer eat a variety of plants.**

## Public Viewing Areas

You may see deer at places that are open to the public. Parks or wildlife refuges in your area may have deer you can observe. There are good parks and refuges to see deer in almost every state in the United States. Many parks in Canada also have large deer populations.

You may ask a ranger or park guide about deer when you visit parks and refuges. Rangers and guides can teach you about deer species in the area. They may take you on a tour of areas where deer live.

# Places to See Deer

**1** **Shenandoah National Park,**
**Luray, Virginia:**
Large populations of white-tailed deer live throughout this park.
The park also offers a number of nature walks and programs.

**2** **Olympic National Park,**
**Port Angeles, Washington:**
Mule deer and elk live in this park. Visitors often view mule deer
in the park's Hurricane Ridge area.

**3** **Nicolet National Forest,**
**Rhinelander, Wisconsin:**
Many white-tailed deer live throughout this park. Visitors may
observe them near trails and campground areas.

**4** **Rocky Mountain National Park,**
**Estes Park, Colorado:**
Mule deer and elk live throughout
this park. Moose live in the
park's western regions.

**5** **Jasper National Park,**
**Jasper, Alberta, Canada:**
Mule deer, elk, moose, and caribou
live in this park.

**6** **White Mountain National Forest,**
**Laconia, New Hampshire:**
Moose and white-tailed deer live in
this park. Moose mainly live in the
northern areas of the park.

**7** **Kerrville-Schreiner State Park,**
**Kerrville, Texas:**
More white-tailed deer live in Texas than any other
state. This park offers excellent opportunities to view
white-tailed deer.

*Chapter 4*

# Making Observations

You may observe deer or deer signs. Deer signs show that deer live in an area. These signs include tracks, droppings, and tree markings.

## Tracks

Look for deer tracks when you go deer watching. You may see tracks in the snow during winter. You may see tracks in mud or soft dirt during spring, summer, and fall. Some people think deer tracks look like hearts. Adult white-tailed and mule deer tracks are about 2.5 to 3.5 inches (6.4 to 8.9 centimeters) long.

**Binoculars can help you observe deer.**

Learn how to tell deer tracks apart. Moose and elk tracks are shaped like mule and white-tailed deer tracks. But moose and elk tracks are larger. Adult moose and elk tracks are about 5 to 6.5 inches (13 to 17 centimeters) long. Measure the tracks you find with a ruler. This will help you decide which type of deer made the tracks.

## Deer Scat

You may find deer droppings. These droppings are called scat. Look for small, round pellets. You may find scat in piles during spring and summer. Each pellet is about .75 inch (1.9 centimeters) long.

Observe deer scat closely. You may be able to tell how long ago a deer was in the area. Fresh deer scat usually is black. Older scat turns brown. Do not touch deer scat with your hands. This can spread disease.

## Tree Markings

Look carefully at trees along trails. Bucks sometimes rub their foreheads and antlers

**You may observe deer tracks or scat.**

against trees. Their fur may stick to the bark of trees. Bucks often make scratches on tree trunks with their antlers. These scratches are called rubs.

Look for tree trunks stripped of their bark. Deer may eat tree bark or low branches during winter when food is scarce.

## Camouflage

You may have trouble seeing deer. Deer have camouflage coloring. Their colors blend into their surroundings. Camouflage coloring helps deer hide from predators.

Both white-tailed and mule deer have red-brown fur during summer. This coloring helps deer blend with the trees and land in forests. Their fur turns blue-gray during winter. This coloring helps deer blend with snow and other winter surroundings. Deer that live in warmer climates may be a shade of brown year-round.

Bucks make rubs on trees with their antlers.

## White-Tailed and Mule Deer Differences

It can be difficult to tell white-tailed and mule deer apart. They look similar. Both of these deer species live in western parts of North America.

There are some differences between white-tailed and mule deer. White-tailed deer hold their tails up when they become startled. Mule deer keep their tails down. Mule deer have a black stripe or patch on the tips of their tails. White-tailed deer have fluffy white tails. White-tailed deer run smoothly. Mule deer keep their legs stiffer than white-tailed deer as they run. Mule deer are larger and have bigger ears than white-tailed deer.

## Recording Your Observations

You may want to record your observations about deer. Make recordings after deer leave your area. Deer may notice your movements if you make notes while they are nearby.

You can record many different deer observations. Note deer sizes and behaviors.

**White-tailed deer hold their tails up when they run.**

Write down what the deer ate. Note where you found the deer. Note the time and location of your observations. Make notes about deer tracks or scat. You also can make drawings of your observations. You may want to make casts of deer tracks.

You also can take photographs of deer or their signs. Move very slowly when you use your camera. You do not want deer to notice you.

Deer watching can be a fun experience. It also can help you learn about the wildlife in your area. Make different observations each time you go deer watching. Over time, you will learn a great deal about deer and the habitats in which they live.

You can record your observations about deer in a notebook.

## White-Tailed Deer

**Description:** White-tailed deer are
the most common deer in North
America. White-tailed deer have a
white patch on their throats. The
underside of their tails also is white.
White-tailed deer often raise their
tails when they are startled.

Male white-tailed deer usually
weigh between 75 and 300 pounds
(34 and 136 kilograms). Females
usually weigh between 50 and 200
pounds (23 and 91 kilograms). The
largest white-tailed deer live in
northern areas of North America.
The smallest type of white-tailed
deer are key deer. Key deer usually
weigh between 45 and 75 pounds
(20 and 34 kilograms). They live
only in the Florida Keys region of
southern Florida. Key deer are
endangered. This means they are in
danger of dying out.

**Habitat:** Deserts, swamps, forests,
fields, prairies, meadows, near
rivers, streams, or lakes

**Food:** Grasses, shrubs, buds, leaves,
acorns, berries; tree bark and twigs
during winter

= Range

# Mule Deer

**Description:** Mule deer live in western regions of North America. These deer have a black tip on their tails. Their large ears have black edges. Mule deer often have white throats and chins.

Male mule deer usually weigh between 125 and 400 pounds (56 and 181 kilograms). Females usually weigh between 100 and 200 pounds (45 and 91 kilograms). The largest mule deer live in the Rocky Mountains. Some mule deer are called black-tailed deer. These deer live in the northwestern regions of North America and along the Pacific Coast. Mule deer can survive in extreme cold climates better than very hot climates.

**Habitat:** Hilly and mountainous areas, deserts, meadows, forests, valleys, plains, prairies, fields

**Food:** Leaves, buds, flowers, fruit, shrubs, grasses

■ = Range

# Elk

**Description:** Most North American elk live in western regions of the continent. Elk are the second largest members of the deer family. Males usually weigh between 800 and 1,100 pounds (363 and 499 kilograms). Females usually weigh about 600 pounds (272 kilograms). Elk have long fur around their necks. Elk colors vary from dark brown to light tan. They usually have a light tan rump patch. Their legs and necks often are darker than their body color.

Elk usually live in herds. This helps protect elk from predators. At least one elk stays alert to sense signs of predators while other animals in the herd eat. Elk often migrate long distances between their summer and winter ranges. Most elk that live in the mountains during spring and summer migrate to lower areas in the winter. Elk sometimes share their living areas with cattle. They usually do not live near people. Elk often vocally communicate with each other.

**Habitat:** Meadows, forests, mountains, near rivers and lakes

**Food:** Grasses, shrubs, leaves, berries, herbs

= **Range**

# Moose

**Description:** Moose are the largest members of the deer family. Males usually weigh between 1,200 and 1,600 pounds (544 and 726 kilograms). Females usually weigh between 800 and 1,300 pounds (363 and 590 kilograms). Male moose have a different antler shape than other deer. Their antlers are spoon-shaped with points on the ends. Moose usually are a shade of brown. They have a large flap of skin called a bell that hangs from their throats.

**Habitat:** Forests, near rivers and lakes

**Food:** Leaves, buds, shrubs, grasses, berries, plants in water; tree bark and twigs during winter

■ = **Range**

# Caribou

**Description:** Caribou live in northern parts of North America. Caribou sometimes are called reindeer. Male caribou usually weigh about 400 pounds (181 kilograms). Female caribou usually weigh about 300 pounds (136 kilograms). Caribou often live in herds. These herds may include more than 100,000 caribou. Both male and female caribou grow antlers. Caribou usually are brown with white or cream on their underparts, necks, and legs. They are excellent swimmers.

**Habitat:** Forests, mountains, river valleys

**Food:** Moss, leaves, shrubs, grasses, mushrooms, fungus on rocks and trees

■ = **Range**

# Words to Know

**adapt** (uh-DAPT)—to change in order to live in a different environment

**blind** (BLINDE)—a place that allows people to hide from animals to observe them

**browser** (BROUZ-ur)—an animal that eats tender shoots, leaves, and twigs of plants

**buck** (BUHK)—a male deer older than 1 year

**doe** (DOH)—a female deer older than 1 year

**fawn** (FAWN)—a deer younger than 1 year

**migrate** (MYE-grate)—to move from one area to another as the seasons change

**range** (RAYNJ)—geographic region where a plant or animal species naturally lives

**rub** (RUB)—the tree markings a buck makes with its antlers

**velvet** (VEL-vit)—the soft, short fur that forms on antlers as they grow

# To Learn More

**Burnie, David.** *Mammals.* Eyewitness Explorers. New York: DK Publishing, 1998.

**La Tourrette, Joe.** *The National Wildlife Federation's Wildlife Watcher's Handbook: A Guide to Observing Animals in the Wild.* New York: Henry Holt, 1997.

**Patent, Dorothy Hinshaw.** *Deer and Elk.* New York: Clarion Books, 1994.

**Russo, Monica.** *Watching Nature: A Beginner's Field Guide.* New York: Sterling Publishing, 1998.

**Zwaschka, Michael.** *The White-Tailed Deer.* Wildlife of North America. Mankato, Minn.: Capstone Press, 1997.

# Useful Addresses

**Canadian Wildlife Service**
Environment Canada
351 St. Joseph Boulevard
Hull, Quebec  K1A 0H3
Canada

**National Key Deer Refuge**
P.O. Box 430510
Big Pine Key, FL  33043

**Quality Deer Management Association**
P.O. Box 227
Watkinsville, GA  30677

# Internet Sites

**North American Animals**
http://www.exn.net/main/reserve/na

**Quality Deer Management Association**
http://www.qdma.com

**Rocky Mountain Elk Foundation**
http://www.rmef.org/index.htm

**U.S. Fish and Wildlife Service**
http://www.fws.gov

**Wildlife Forever**
http://www.wildlifeforever.org

**The Wildlife Management Institute**
http://www.jwdc.com/wmi/main.html

# Index

DEMCO

599.65 Bai
Bair, Diane.
Deer watching

STONY CREEK
ELEMENTARY LIBRARY